Things I Blindly Took As Gospel

Beau Williams

Things I Blindly Took As Gospel

Beau Williams

Waterside Productions.
Cardiff, CA

2021

Printed in the United States of America

First Printing, 2021

ISBN-13: 978-1-951805-64-7 print edition.
Things I Blindly Took As Gospel. Beau Williams.
Cover photo by Robyn Nicole Film and Photo
https://robynnicolefilmandphoto.com
Jacket Layout by Beau Williams
Interior Layout by Beau Williams

Waterside Productions

Waterside Productions
2055 Oxford Ave
Cardiff, CA 92007
www.waterside.com

This book is dedicated to my sister, SunMi: the coolest
person I know.

Table of Contents

PART TWO
//
EURO COINS, POCKET KNIVES, AND OTHER TYPES OF GODS

PART THREE
//
MASKS

The following poems have been published previously in their current or earlier versions:

When I Die: Quarantine Poetry from Across the Pond. Skeptipol.com, 03/28/2020

Locks and Latches: Quarantine Poetry from Across the Pond. Skeptipol.com, 03/28/2020.

Call the Locksmith: University College Cork. Creative Corona, 04/07/2020.

FOREWORD

Beau Williams is family in the sense that we are not related but together we have shared holy spaces; a dive bar in Boston, a coffee shop in New Hampshire, a theatre at the National Poetry Slam. These are poetry churches we held the same hushed breath inside of, learning at the altar of exceptional craft, our laughter a new kind of worship. We have also each scattered across oceans to fall in love in new countries, whispered the American prayer 'the cops don't carry guns here' in relief, fallen asleep thousands of miles from those who raised us.

What I mean is, there is a loneliness you have to dig yourself out of when everyone you love and left behind only sees your new life through a screen. To read Things I Took Blindly as Gospel is to unearth pain and learn from it, to point to the wound and say *I survived that*.

These poems are rich dirt in capable hands, swallowing what has come before and nurturing what has yet to be born. Beau is unafraid to examine the very stillness we breathe in with the kind of resilience I believe only New England could breed. With tenderness of craft, sharp imagery, and hope, Beau skillfully leads us not out of but through the darkness as he unearths a city's tenderness and grit, guiding us through the splintered alleyways of Ireland.

There is a truth, a raw gullible emotion, when you write about a new home, searching for where you might belong even though you will always be too foreign — forever changed by the choice you made to leave. And perhaps this suits Beau - to confront his demons, to find his voice in a new country, speaking to what everyone feels but has never said. These poems remind me that the kindness of a stranger can change the course of a whole day; that as each of us tries to dig ourselves out of our loneliness, we are not alone.

I am delighted now for you, dear reader, to dive into Beau Williams' newest collection of work, and to lean into the storm.

With warmth,
Carrie Rudzinski, Author of *The Shotgun Speaks*

"These words are wounds that I am grateful for."

-Wil Gibson

"If you're writing letters to the prisoners
start tearing down the bars
If you're handing out flashlights in the dark
start handing out stars."

-Andrea Gibson, *Say Yes.*

"This wine is awful. Get me another glass."
-Moira Rose

PART ONE

Rusted Locks, Empty Pints, and Dying in Your Sleep

NOTIFICATION

It's 2 in the afternoon
and this room is a warm
ceramic bowl.
My cell phone blinks beside me
like taillights that gnash
and click from atop a hill.

My arm knows this reach well,
this weighted strain.
I want to pluck
my thumb from my hand,
to stamp it down
a sewer grate.

The window shade
is half drawn,
the room has become
a white-hot light
against the shadowed.

I'm sick of digging for God
in the devil's mouth
but those teeth remind me, still,
of a cave of crosses.

Here, in my bed,
if only for distraction,
I would string my tattoos
together with sewing thread.
I'd dig under the base of the ink
on my hip and peel them off
together in a thick ribbon. I wish
to allow myself to writhe.

To turn the bed a clotted red,
and, still,
I'd reach for a star
that will flash forever
as it falls.

SEPTEMBER 23RD

Of course, that misted hair
would unfold down her shoulders;
wild twisted staircase she is.
Struck me weak in the guts
of a parade through town.

How humbled the band must have been
to warm her shadow in the rain.
How alone that crowd must have
felt around us.

Her eyes reached from behind
that mess of rusted locks,
caught me dumbstruck with no key.

My heart is now an apple in my throat.
She took a bite
and my knees buckled
the way you unawaredly do
when the taxi picks you up to take you home.

WASH THE KNIFE THAT CUT THE LIMES

A leather jacket holds a lit Marb Light
between her Claddagh ring and middle finger
where the palm makes a cup.
It smokes itself out.

She orders a virgin mojito
as if she demands he disrobe.
He forgets to smack the mint.
How disappointing.

She knows she's got a man back home
less boy than this whole city
can shake its dick at.
Knows he knows exactly how
to make the garnish sweat.
Barkeep finishes too quick
but the drink still tingles her tongue.
He won't charge her.
She don't pay easy.

Leather jacket puts the cigarette to her lips,
sucks the smoke back to cherry
as the exit door grows claws
then bites them down
quick as they came.

LOVE OVER SLEEP IN THE EARLY MORNING

Luck moaned a scratch of jealousy as we
snuck under the lamppost on the corner of Cross
and Shop Street to kiss. The boozehounds tossed
their Buckfast bottles and pants down the alley.

Bare bones of the night rattle as rain sheets
land hard like windowpanes around us. We are lost
keys in a back pocket. Our rum mouths, glossed
across each other's faces. Silent the wind of the city

jostle all the plastic from trees; float them to land.
We didn't watch the moonlight glare,
see shadows play the night. We just stood there
washed out and happy. You grabbed my hand,

crossed the street through dirty puddles. We struck
free then danced home together in the muck.

DROOL

I rolled over in the night and caught you
asleep, mouth open, drool collected in
the pocket of your cheek. If it's the good
sleep, the drip will come. It will puddle on

the pillow and you'll dream of bumblebees
and soft days. I'll store the silly moments
in my memories. I can sift through these
when I wake on the floor in tight knots, since

I seldom get lost, but I do get lost.
You've brought me back from the swill of the bar
when I was less of a flower, more wasp.
You plant daisies where the garden is dark.

I like you. You woke, slurped, and laughed. I said
you were cute. You told me to go to bed.

HEAVY

Hooded beings flock
into my room while I'm asleep,
turn my body petrified,
run their boney fingers down the walls
and all the pictures turn to ash.

One shadow stands above me,
eyes like smoldered fire pits,
while other shadows crawl
onto my chest.
My body is a heavy gutted tree.

Two more shadows
gather at my side.
The rain will build
outside my walls and
wash whatever
god of sleep
there is
into the night.

ONE THING I KNOW FOR SURE IS THAT IF I CAN OPEN MY EYES, I AM FREE

This morning I died alone with my eyes wide open.
The rest of me was a wet towel on branches,
My heart: cramped from trying.
Of every truly dead thing that has yet to

   jolt awake,
      how many know this weight?

How many watch their lovers
collapse over them and sob?
How many stare at an empty room for weeks?
How many hear their killers leave the room
or feel the cold
sheet drape them?

How many watch the clouds brush   past
      as the scared cop phones an alibi?

Of the dead-as-we-know-them,
do they mock us at their wake?
Do they rest comfortably in padded maple,
get butterflies as they're lowered into the ground?

What percentage scream each passing
second into the empty mouth of God
as evidence against death?

Against everything we thought it was;
against movies and sacred stories
and every well-thumbed rosary bead?

How many know the coroner's scalpel?

Hear the incinerator door clink,
latch shut, feel the new flames
lick their rigid bodies dry?

WHILE YOU WERE AT WORK

From the branch outside our bedroom window,
a pigeon squawks. If it could open wide enough,
                       I'd snatch him,

stuff him under my pillow, hold the pillow   taut.

Feathers would erupt,
would rise into the air,
would seem to stay there,
each hollow bone's attempt to fly away. Beneath,
my guest would roll, would thump   in   place,
would give this bed a heartbeat and maybe
we could breathe again.

My pigeon friend would claw and peck a patch
to burrow down below but know that
in his heart, his wings were never
built to dig this deep.

CALL ME WHEN YOU GET HOME SAFE

We didn't kiss on the bridge in the rain
that night. I was made of tequila and you
were long fingers reaching. You were good
to me and bad to be around. The streets

were empty, save sounds of lovers making
lover-sounds behind us, save the bits of
sober me all tangled in my veins, save
all my many eyes. You waited for me to

make the move. I had everything to lose
and a gut of urges, gnawing. The grain
of me in the glare of your eye was as
bold as I'd ever be. You told me not

to worry, it was just a little fun.
We didn't kiss and the promised streetlights
sizzled on. The river continued to
take the rain and the rain-soaked city spun.

AFTERWARDS, YOU SHOWERED

and maybe you finished.
Maybe you sat under the water
pressure and wept, made a grocery list:
your meditative chore, your welcome bother.

Did you reach up, turn the red knob to blast,
let the steam build to burn again?
Did you finger your name on the shower glass?
Did you pick a clump of hair from the drain,

hold it to the light, watch the water drip thru?
Did you palm the wad on the tile?
Have you prayed for something new?
Have the bones inside you itched a while?

Perhaps you closed your eyes, cut my face
from the act then came, came with a violent grace.

AFTER LAST NIGHT

I've woken with a belly washed and soon
the dryness in my eyes will set. The Powers
bottle gutted on the counter holds a note.
The mirror on the closet door: an excuse

we tied a blanket to. We lost the moon
again. Pocketed again with all the hours.
Trampled and danced on all the flowers.
Let the bottle hum a hollow tune.

Can't we let our hollow bodies be,
we sacks of bones and bourbon?
Maybe every bit of paint
to peel or storm to lock a latch to isn't stiff

enough a drink to stand a night on. Maybe
cobwebs aren't the mistletoe to bite
a bottle under. Sobriety:
a letter in a bottle set adrift.

EACH NIGHT

Netflix beat and beat its body
against the computer screen
as my room got dark and darker.

What moonlight crawled in through the window
sparred with blue light punches, swung.
Sitting on my bed, I never thought to close my eyes
for seven episodes, so the screened in devils reached
and scratched and caught them.

Should have seen me hold true, Hero of Lethargy.
I didn't flinch once.
Not when the claws hooked my eyelids.
Not when the veins cracked red through the whites
and I cried a bit of blood. Didn't finch,
but I pulled my hand into my sleeve,
wiped away the battle proof before it dried to my cheeks.

A face paint written in another language.
One I've been trying to translate for you
but my clothes keep coming back with stains.

MAYBE READ SOMETHING HAPPY BEFORE BED

Jack Torrence haunted a boy
down the hall last night,
limped a roque mallet
along the carpet; tapped the walls.
I slept restless
under a book full of bodies.

My brain etched a horror story
to the inside of my skull
to be read backwards in a mirror.
I lit candles in my dreams
by which to decipher it, but the
Colorado snowstorms blew them out.

In my bed in Dublin,
I flailed through the night
to edge the hammer swings and
hallways drenched in blood.
My lover woke up groggy with her
hand pressed to my chest.

Her face hung on its bones,
she was smiling.
I woke embarrassed, apologized
again, to my heart.
She kissed me and told me
she held me through it

until my muscles thawed and
I became less of a frayed wire.
I know that I will love my love
until I am a hotel made of ghosts.
We will defeat monsters together
and we will somehow shine-on,
                    shine-on.

BACKLIT

Her chandelier heart hangs the way
a car dangles from a cliff edge.
It blinks off-beat, shows the wires and cast iron
that keeps the beast from falling.

Beyond that, her lungs hung on a wall,
black as tar and bullet-holed.
It used to smell of gasoline,
used to shred rubber up the California coast.
It's backlit now, mostly for show,
but it still smokes its cigarettes to the bone.

There's a memory somewhere,
sprawled out on the stone,
the image of a sandcastle on the beach.
Sweetly made with decorative window frames
and detailed spiral towers.
It's since been covered with a towel,
knocked flat and blasted by old heaters.

Sometimes God is the sun and
prayer is to stare into it.
Sometimes we get an answer
without going blind and
sometimes God is a TV in the rain.

Your wings were always tucked away
between your body and the dream.
Lit up and beaming brave,
how often do our wings mimic our hearts?
Both unfurl to catch, then ride, a breeze
or make their own.
How many lovers wish their hearts

and wings were more than flashing lights.

How many wish to peel our skin
and fold it like a sweater,
to set it in the center of the room,
 and shine a spotlight on the mess?

What is left once we've stripped
the metal from our throats,
the wires from our brains?

How bold a soul is she who hands
her voice to a stranger in the rain?

GONE
For Demeter

Your voice tore through the wind again,
a storm I threw myself into.
I thrashed in the thorns of it all.

As it passed, I reached for you. I
missed. Caught only seeds and nothing.
The trees are now a stoic calm.

and me: a crumpled thing,
a haggard blueberry patch.
My throat, a fist of shredded grass.

Beetles tick around inside my
sandy tangled mane. I will freeze
when the ice comes through. I will freeze

with both eyes open.

HANGMAN

Cold breeze hangs in the air.
Kicks its feet until it doesn't.
This city holds no memorials for dead gods.
Corked my heart in whisky bottles;
left them in the heat of day,
'til they went bad.

Bottles broke when the sun popped.
Sounded like a child ripped from a tree.
The burst sun swiped my knavish hands,
built shadows broad as wind.
The children scoop their broken bones,
collect their tired frames and wander.
Hive themselves away in the cavern pocket
of the fresh-hanged god.

If I could grant one wish,
it would brown an apple's bruise.
It would turn inside my mouth.
Clouds like tongues would swell and tear.
I would kiss my lover in the spitting rain.

JUPITER'S CONDITION

You drool when you sleep the good sleep.
The barman smacks the counter and you're up,
bar mat pasted to your cheek.
He calls you by your name and you stumble from
the spirited place you'd been.

You grab your coat and somehow find the door.
The rain drops in buckets outside but only when you're in
it.
It's dark as death out there, too.
The door is heavy and it locks behind you.

ANOTHER TIME I WISHED YOU WERE HERE

A happy baby cackled down the hall.
The starter shriek: a cry or joyful bell
that became a stuttered laughter clap.

The exclamation turned
the people in the lobby
and reception desk to goose fat.
Everyone melted.
Everyone looked up
from their crosswords
or coffee to catch the ham
and a woman in the next room
caught a rainbow in an oyster shell.
This hotel became a bouquet.

Neatly wrapped chocolate
fell from the ceiling
and all of our wallets
filled with cash.
Every rug was a magic carpet,
if you were here,
it would float us.
Every mirror had our names
inscribed with lipstick.

- XOXO-

The news came on and
the President resigned.
Mother Nature got a foot rub
in the Master Suite
and she cooled back down.

The swimming pool was
deep with acceptance letters
and the cure for cancer.
The bellboy paid off all our debt.

I closed my eyes and imagined all things good.

The break in the clouds
blew over the sun,
It filled the hall
with light for one
warm moment
before it drew itself

back closed.

LATE TO DINNER

The dull knife slid off the onion's back,
dug a sickle through my nail.
A pearl of blood
gathered at the base,
this wet bulb drawn from a tap.
A cat's tongue yawned out.

A white calm took the room
before the sting sang through
and a soft moon swelled red quick;
the kind of gash a cat or god
could crawl into to watch.
I licked the moon clean
then held it to my shirt.
What a dirty star to pray to;
this hasty glimpse of heaven, carved.

I tied the wound too tight with tape
and carried on chopping big things
into little ones.

HOLDING HANDS AND SKIPPING STONES

Crocodile Rock fills the air
as the woman I love more than
music makes dinner. She cuts
broccoli from redwoods to stir fry
in our tiny apartment.

She has mastered the art
of wielding a blade
with the precision
of a salsa dancer.
Her hips are a tire swing
in a breeze.

I sit useless on the bed in the kitchen,
writing poetry to Elton John
as he tells us about the biggest
kick he ever got.
My pen pushes through the page
as she turns
the kitchen
into a Rock and Roll synagogue
and she knows
every single word.

CROSS YOUR HEART

I know the delete button,
a piece of my rib hidden beneath it.
I pick the button from my phone-
finger the bone.
Feels like the broken tooth I used to tongue,
a warm body on a cold screen.
Feels like a car, been crunched with a man inside.
A wedding ring pulled from a corpse.

I can only write poems now
on the floor
in a corner
in the dark
with a pen.

I can only write poems
with my heart
asleep on the bed.

This room is sometimes a casket
and sometimes a cloud.
When I write,
it becomes
a locket for bones.
An elephant graveyard
to be tucked in my pocket
or hung from my neck,
will weigh heavy on my chest.

When I cough the dry cough,
I split open
and a crumpled car
tumbles
or my ribs pour out like glass.
I build a truth on my tongue that
beats at the back, that
beats at the back, that
beats itself numb at the back
of my teeth like a drum.

BREAKING OUT OF SLEEP PARALYSIS

It's never the shriek of the car alarms
that wakes her. Isn't the herald flashes
of our broken oven blinking brave, my
molars gnawed to dust, or the prickly wind.

She sleeps like a stone in a creek. She can
flinch or yawn or twist at her body's will.
She can wake from hollowness or dream through
open dreams, but her mind is always sharp.

When I wake before my body does, I
notice my slow breaths first. How they rest inside
the bag of me, reach once or twice between
eternities. I notice my heartbeat

second. How it quickens when caught off-guard.
Thirdly, my bones are axel rods tossed in
a heap strapped to the bed. I die each night
inside myself to the grunge of car alarms,

of ever-howling winds. I grind my jaws
and force a plea. It comes out a distant
drone. Somehow it always slices through the
tight lips and dreams and shakes her alive

enough to press a hand to me and shove.
A thrust to rock me out of this paralysis,
enough to rip new breath into my lungs,
to belly-up a nightmare,
to shock a bell well-rung.

HER RED HAIR

It clogs the shower drain.
Our children's children will wear it well
and yours will be a faded marigold by then.
In this moment, it is strung around the flat.
Bits of orange angel feathers fallen.
Hidden strands glistening to greet me
when the sun hits it just right.
I will gladly pull them string by string
from crevasses for the rest of my days.

A WET RING

spots the bar top.
I set the bottle down again,
twist to make another ring.
Repeat until the bottle runs dry.
Barkeep wipes my practice
runs with a rag
then tosses me a bar mat.

Gutter flowers grow lush in the rain.
      The streets outside begin to drown
           and the ditches start to sing.

My lover is in the loo,
 no doubt scrolling through
pictures of wedding gowns.
I fiddle with the stone
in my pocket. Run
my finger round the band
and slip it through, then out again.

She loves me with a bumblebee heart:
curious, lively,brave.
I love her like
the planet has a chance.

She makes her way
back across the room.
I think of all the busted things
that healed themselves
to land me here.
She buzzes back
to the seat I saved for her

and the sidewalk dandelions
matches pitch.

My heart is cumbersome in my chest
like a man knelt down in a busy place.
I fight to keep my words
from being fallen rain
as her eyes break
                a sweet cloud
                over us both.

PART TWO

Euro Coins, Pocket Knives and Other Types of Gods

NEST

Curl up here with the angels.
Make rest alongside the bottles,
whole and broke.
Sleep if your body asks.
Jump when it won't.

ECHOES IN THE ALLEY

Galway bars'll pull you
a perfect pint or a shit one.
You'll come back either way
the way a bad love
or a good one will.

Other towns'd be
too white a cloud
to write a decent song about
the rain.
The city where all the clouds are made
is grey as streets
of cobblestone.

Come find
the batch of
lonely hearts
all locked away
up Quay Street.
Come join the fruitless search
for Sonny Casey's
missing shoes.

Buskers, here, pay rent off
noise complaints
and get waterlogged.
The ukulele players
shred their fingertips
as if a little blood would be enough
to keep the sun
awake a little more.

The drummers beat cajons

until the bottles
that we hide our secrets in
all shatter in our guts.
We drink
until the bar top starts to twist:
a rickety bridge
we'll gladly lose a couple hours to.

It's loud until it's done
and nobody's seen
Woody Murphy since Thursday.
This city is a wild rain.
This city lost its phone last night
and the clouds all rippled silver.
It's smoked a million cigarettes
and saved as many souls.
It weaves its fingers
through guitar strings
like other people's belt loops.

This city has another
twisted ankle;
a gnarled root
erupting from the street.
We drunken fools and heroes
all have hooked a foot
and bit the pavement;

all been lifted up by friends
and shaken clean
before the blood
could leave a stain.

AT RUXTON COURT

There is a tunnel entrance
that swallows boys on the street,
slurs them
            across   our   yard.

Poor girls, pulled in,
get spit out our   end
when the night runs low on
rumors.

The courtyard is full of falling children
with blisters on heels,
rollies in fists, or both
with a tongue in their throats.

If the echoes flown 'round
        these stones were birds,
        they would weave between us,
        pick at loose threads, catch us
undone at our
            doorsteps.

TULIP BULB

[A dare wherein a person
stuffs a lightbulb into his mouth]

Smooth glass, frail, fights a bit but if
he can stretch his jaw fit to crack,
the bulb should slide right in.
The easy part is done. The trick is in the extraction.

The human mouth is built to take it in.
The teeth prevent the pull-out.
His eyes will grow round
and white with fear as the situation sinks in.

There are two ways for sure to save him:
        break the jaw near the temple's hinge,
        or with a heavy tool begin
        to knock the glass to petals.

Hold the screw part steady.
Lightly tap the glass above,
careful not to knick the teeth.
                Once the bottom part is severed,
                find a thin screwdriver. Have him
                hang his head so none of the
                shards are swallowed.
Guide the metal into the
fragile flower of his mouth.
Lightly tap the base of the tool
to pierce the round. With luck,
slivers won't enter the throat.
                With more luck, the globe will crack
                to grabbable shards,
                easy enough to extract.

Most likely, gentle tapping
against the sides will be necessary.
Break them into bits to then be
pinched and gently yanked,

one bloody petal at a time.

POCKET KNIFE
From a Nymph named Echo

You were face down in your face,
            drowned in your own eyes and you
will be remembered forever and ever.
            I am ever only everything you said
until another lover comes along,
            and howls like you did like they do.
If I had had a will or pocket knife, I
            could have taken out your throat and
taken out your throat and taken out
            your throat and we would have survived.

OAK TREES

It is winter morning, still.
The watermark of the moon's
got its hands in its pockets.
There is a blackbird nest in
the tree's chest outside,
so still, its big dead, big grey heart.
This street is lined with skeletons
that I call by the wrong name:
oak, birch, inside joke.
I name them after the living
things back home.

All the bags of bones here die randomly,
back home they freeze when it's time,
then they thaw in the Spring with the daisies.
I've yet to give this town a chance,
still act like I've got somewhere else to be.

Yesterday, the guy from the laundromat
said *Hi* like he knew me
and it carried me through 'til sundown.
I try to cup this town in my hands
but it drains through and wets my shoes.
I write poems and they char in the Big Smoke
or get carried away up the Liffey.
Everything in Winter dies.
I've forgotten how to be a ghost.

I forgot to learn the names of trees.

They couldn't care less
They just bark down and show me
their collarbones without even trying.
I'd like to show them mine too
or read them a poem
but they're gone with the warmth
and the songbirds 'til Spring.

They'll do what they do
and won't owe me a thing.
Maybe dead things are dead things
'cause that's what they do best.
I have a blacked-out notebook
and a nest in my chest
Makes a faint Autumn beat
                     beat
                       beat
that raps at my Fallen bones.

Maybe this is where I learn
to shine the grime off my shoes.
Maybe this is where I reach
for the hands of the moon.

SLOW FOR A FRIDAY

The table in the back has rings of wet
and wobbles when you touch it
so you don't.
Then you do.
Then you don't.
Then you laugh.
An abandoned cityscape of bottles with
half-picked labels, half-drunk. The lips
that gripped them earlier now hold a smoke or
conversation back away from thirsty ears.

None of those drinks belong to you.
You trace a coaster between them all.

      not touching
               not touching

         not touching.

You are overpoured and teeter
near this city made of glass.

Barkeep is also drunk with
      (or near)
the cigarette girls.

He leans his heavy body
across the counter and
reaches for a hand,

      (not touching
         not touching
            not touching)

whispers things
that make them laugh
like he's the only person
in the room.

FOR THE FAIRIES AND THE STONES

Down the wet fishbone of an ally,
a boy belts out a tune
he uncorked from his father's jug.

> "Never thought I'd lose you here.
> Never thought you'd find your way".

Plays loud to the bricks, and the stone,
and the fairies who dance in the rain.
One spins another on the tails of a Euro Coin.
One sits on a cigarette butt, taps her foot and
smokes one.
The boy knows this song like he knows hands.
Boy's veins pump legend.
His throat grows an oak tree.

The tree gives birth to birds.
They fall from branches,
turn to bottle caps
before they bounce into cracks in the street,
before they bite into the undersole
of whatever dazzled folk might stumble by.

A WAY TO SKIN A CATCALLER

She turned around
to face the boys
and every tongue
among them
tied in knots.
Her voice: a blue flame rolling,
a shotgun blast,
scattered flock of crows,
every night the keys
she wraps around her fist,
a wall of legs
and clavicle and woman toppled
over me to silence
out the Buckfast Boys.
She knew, too well, the limp,
the drag of a drunkard's
jaw along the hinge of himself.

What I never told the boys
in the street in the nights
turned to pebbles in my mouth.
These are the moments we've
told the world we'd be there for.
The idea of us
playing hero or
being anything more.
A scene where my body moves
instead of a still
where my body breaks.
The woman will make us
believe she has swallowed the moon
by swallowing the moon.

The boys behind me howl
at the rip in the sky and not
one of us will ever hear
our own voice.

AGENCY
for Cyntonia Brown

Skin from the head of a fresh stag drips
where its body hangs on twigs and rocks
and teeth of dogs. Fur in parts, a human hand
with fingers nearly hooves. One eye: fragile,
popped, and one a thick glass bowl.
Goddess rids the dogs when the threat dies.
She breathes in, sinks below the water,

presses her eyes closed, allows her hair
to rest atop the surface like dropped leaves,
spilt blood, clothes on the floor to lure
a pack of hungry mouths from the woods.

She lifts her head to catch the light sun.
Warm silence begins to perch around the bones.

WHEN YOU'VE SWALLOWED A TYPHOON
or
THE CITY BUSES HAVE NEVER HAD TOILETS
AND I SHOULD KNOW THAT BY NOW

The 140 bus was stuck in traffic
near O'Connell Street.
The block was flooded with people.
The spire was an unfurled paper clip
that touched the sky.

We hadn't moved in many hours
or a few breaths
and my bladder was
a horse head in my lap.

They poured in through the opened door.
Rocked the bus steadily.
Each *beep* followed by kind eyes,
grins grown like flowers across their faces
and I wanted to snip them.

My legs were crossed,
bladder kicked the guts of me,
an animal dropped in a pool.
Flailed hooves lurched
and reaching for any way out.

BLUE LIGHTS

Night busses have blue
lights that make it hard for folks
to shoot up on the ride.
Turns their veins invisible,
so they say.

I remember this and
hold, upright, the underbelly of my arm.
The veins are there, though dull as brush
strokes. I could find them if I needed to.

I could dig in, tug at them like pull-cords.
Could pluck them out of me then snap
them back to place: one, two, again.
There would be no blood in this blue light.
Just doughy skin to work. This bus,

near empty, loses people every hour
between where we were and where we mean
to be.

WATCHED POT
On Registering with Immigration

The garda station fills with water.
We pace the hall in wet socks.
We carry patient bones.

Somebody's boss grew white hair quick.
Tells us all we've read the wrong books;
to come back later.

We stay. Grind our teeth. Scuff our shoes,
swallow our last piece of gum.

Behind a wall, the pipe bursts and the plaster starts to
bubble.
stairwells creak with the weight of us there,
of paperwork piles, of waterlogged men from elsewhere.

Boss man builds a rowboat
fills it with the right books.
Plucks the pages out like single
tissues from a box
             drops
               them in the   water
          up above us

as we watch.

ETHAN HAWKE MIGHT HAVE SLEPT HERE
Legends of a Parisian Bookshop

The walls are made of books on shelves.
Rows of spines are tiny bones
tucked between each other on the racks.
A famous cat sleeps in a large chair all day,
wakes to climb along its paper jungle,
and jump out the window to the rooftop.
He most surely speaks French.

The ones who take their pictures by the
"Please No Picture" sign are surely American.

We and celebrities have passed thru,
grabbed at everything, and faded
into dust on the shelves. Our ghosts
take up space while the cat rolls around
in the haunt of us.

A couple of tiles have chipped or popped
where tourists have pressed their traveled soles.
Rock to tiptoe as they stretch,
                          reach
                                  touch
                          stretch
                                  reach
                                      touch.

FIRST BITE

For a hungry Eurydice

My wrists were too small for lute strings bracelets
or handcuffs. I'll take Hades and a terror in the dark.

I crawled and searched for snakes
in the grass in the field behind the altar.
You've never seen my knees so worn.
The serpents wouldn't strike at first,
such calm creatures. So, I bit one.

I made it here without you. I did this by myself.

You puffed your chest and plucked your lute
and charmed your way to me.

When I send you back, you'll cry, you'll thrive,
and you'll weave my trauma into songs
to fill your bed and belly.

The women up above (oh the women!)
will devour you. Come to me then, shredded.
I am other-worldly here.

THE COURTESY TO TRIP

"When I hesitated, he let the insult fly. Beside me, the men laughed, nervously. Had either of them said anything, he would have been a feminist hero. If I'd said anything, I would have been a bitch."
        -Emilie Pine. *Notes to Self.*

They've set the bar at our feet. We
could trip over it and save the day
but we see it a threat, a sharp fox, a thing
that strikes. We are often right.

To lift a foot would be to fight;
to see another person as a person.
Sure as hell, that lack of sturdy
balance knocks us over every time.

They expect us to fail.
We glass jar of fists.
We hurling pitch of knotted backs.
They are often right

If we spoke up once, the streets would flood
with streamers and elephants and the best
high school brass bands in the state.
Our faces would be slapped on flags
and, with our phones, we'd film them as they
whipped violently to the wind.

IN SEARCH OF SEEDS
Persephone to Zeus

Your godly hand, a salmon on a wrist,
jumps the gap between my teeth, fishes
down my throat. Butts of all the stars
and mountains in your nails. Your fingers
dig and dig blind. Search for any parcel
from the dark. I told you I was clean
and that my body was a barren cave,
but you, a godly god, must make your rules
and lock our jaws with them. You must
turn our bodies hollow for the story of it all.
Big god. Big godly god. You'll find the seeds.
Keep digging, Father. Dig. Dig. Dig.

THE OLD CHURCH TAKES THE STORM

Rain beats itself against the roof
and the roof drinks the body down.
High above, the ceiling sags a wet chest over the pulpit,
       (cracks across it
           are stretch marks ripped through)
drips a rhythm on the cross,
the mimic of tongue clicks
to the backs of teeth.

Water mixed with dust draws
black tears down the heavy holy.

      Tap
      Tap
      Tap
        Drag

Each drop, a swallowed prayer,
paints long fingers down the walls,
grows rust patches where it settles.
Every tall window stained hanged-man blue,
              stained dirty gold,
           stained blood,
fogs until handprints show and reach for ghosts.

      Tap
      Tap
      Tap

Water rises and the carpet takes it in.
Floats torn hymn pages,
floats flies,
floats nimble woven palm leaves.

Bits of ceiling scattered over pews
like dirt over bones.
Heaven wears holes now where rain
or prayers
or breath
or God
or God
or smoke
or heat
can leave.

A weakness biting at its bones.
These dark clouds brought in
start to build.

We watch and wait
for its chest to burst.

FEAR SA TSRUTH
Irish for "Man in the Stream"

Heavy church doors stained with sin
crack open to Sunday.
God puts a wet thumb over the town.
The streets are littered with cigarette butts in heels
and men dipped in the drink.

Around the bend,
boys in loose ties or nooses throw rocks
at yield signs, at bus stop boys,
at shiny cars from away.

Fucking Americans.

A woman in a lived-in body
lives in motion 'cross the bridge,
pushes her baby carriage,
mind set on the sermon
or which mouth eats next.

Small towns in Ireland start with
"Kill" or end in "Moor".
The cops don't carry guns here.
In Galway there is a time of year where
college kids toss their bodies into the river.

Folks don't fear cops here.
Folks fear god.
Folks drink cans like Gods on river duty.
Boys here don't talk about depression
but we can "stop being a *bitch*."

We let loose the night
to a murder of pints.

Jinxes dare us to yell into the alter
that God
that God
that God
may finally wake up
all picked gut and brine,

might wretch into the bay,
might stir the boys' bodies
in the foam like flies
or catch our holy names in the wind.

We pray a savior to unbuckle our jaws,
to balm our shredded lungs,
to unhinge the church doors
to dry them in the sun.

THE DANCE OF DUBLIN
After Hayes after Brooks

We've begun to pack everything into boxes. We
can pick up the keys on Wednesday. A real
realtor, will be there with real keys. How cool
a lean must we goad to save face? We
wrap our knives in old shirts and lift what's left
of ourselves from our past. Let us try to school
fate and spin chance here, this one room palace we
pulled from pocket. Can we watch drunk boys lurk
the city streets from our window, still? On late
nights, will they do the dance we know? Will we
breathe deep in this strange city? Let us strike
matches with our thumbnails and pull, straight,
the curtains when we
sing.

We've buried our sin
in the floorboards of the old house. We
know where to find them, under the thin
board in the kitchen. It still smells of gin
though we bleached it and scrubbed deep. May we
always move with the neighboring pub's jazz.
May our new home and old fuel carry us past June.
May our new stories take us where we
mean to be, cutting tomatoes in a laundry room. We die
when we decide to let the knives dull too soon.

INSTAGRAM POST

My fiancé sits at the other end of the bed,
cross legged, drafting an Instagram post
that will change the world.
She challenges me to check myself
to acknowledge which giant's
shoulders I am standing on
and respect the view.

I consider what it means to be fulfilled.
To see possibility as a paycheck in your hand.
You can wish it to mean power or success
but until you cash it, it's just paper.
What is a paycheck without action?
Ask any matchstick.

She makes me want to imagine the future.
During a pandemic, it's hard
to think past systemic problems
and the weight of the fight
that we're fighting to solve them,
but I close my eyes
be grateful I'm alive
and I see a house in Maine
maybe a front porch that wraps around.
I see a couple of dogs and a cat
and for the first time in forever
I get to hug my mother back.

These rushing thoughts,
carry with them potential.
2020 wasn't some strange, cursed year.
Isolation forced us to roll
back our lips in the mirror and

measure our teeth.

You can't discuss something with no language.
You can't fight something you can't see.
You can't change something that doesn't have a name
and last year we wrote it across the sky.
We tore down skyscrapers to make room for sunsets.
We ripped up abandoned parking lots
and let wildflowers grow next.
We planted pinecones that grew to be
family trees and we are still trying to
process the ax swings
with our big leaves
that grow to eat sunbeams,
but these things take time.

2021 is a year to grow.
2021 is a year to know
what true healing is,
What it means to recognize the rear view
but look forward towards the mountains while we drive.
What it means to be fully alive.
2021 is about taking chances.
Bloom faith and fray hate until it's just
thin strips of wires you can separate
and reshape to spell "I love you".
This year is the year of saying "Yes".
This is the year of the self-check.
This is the year of saying clearly:
"I deserve the best"
because we only get the wishes
that we ask and we work for.

We have a canopy of emotions to
process from the last storm
and this year is the platform.

When we speak,
we are every voice that came before.
When we love with battlefield hearts,
we disassemble the war.
Last year we worked the earth
until our hands gave birth to future.
We are a rosined bow pulled across
the violin vocal cords of the universe.

Watch us play our notes with conviction now.
Let us shake the walls of hatred down
with music. We are music.
We are going to get through this
with a river for a voice and a fist in the air,
with a song in our throats and courage in our stare.

My fiancé might not change the world with a paragraph,
but she challenges me to be less of an epitaph
and more of a sonnet.
I want to acknowledge where I am dirt
and lay a rose petal on it.
I want to see where I hurt
and put a salve on the rawness.
I want to reach for my goals
with my faith as the harness.

This coming year,
watch our dreams write themselves out in cursive
with curls that wrap like front porches in Maine.
Watch us believe in ourselves
and watch the whole world change.
We will unlock our potential.
What's a deadbolt to a stream?
We will withstand the wind.
What's a whisper to
to a Redwood Tree?

SCROLL DOWN

A man climbs atop the bar
the way lighting crawls up a cloud.
Pours liquor into the patrons' waiting mouths.
They sit, faces together with wet lips open,
tongues like beached seals panting.

This is that party-boy fun, that blackout ocean,
that carefree craic that foams from your lips.
This bar is up the way from here and cuts at you
from behind the phone's blue light,
behind the locked door and windows barely cracked.

Scroll down.
Somewhere in China, 10,000 ravers pack together
to dance en mass at a festival and the clouds
open their own throats in celebration.

Scroll down.
In Sturgis, motorcycles cough black tar and
carry bodies to the end of the road.

Scroll down.
In Barcelona, Father Death foots a crowded beach,
tells tourists to walk home or walk into the sea
and the sea breaks shore with a heavy crash.

The outside world is a casket
and we're begging for the final nail.
Hammer swing.
A nightmare isn't a thing with teeth,
it's loved ones that tell you the teeth aren't real.

Scroll down

and Portland is a tumultuous flame.

Scroll down
Dublin spits a bad joke through a mouthful
to a server wearing armour.

Scroll down.
Your hometown is a tequila bottle wrapped in a flag.

Scroll down
and prove our thumbs are anchors,
turn our phones to toothy rocks
that tear into our sides.
Each day we are alive, we are slit open
and we fill the room with water.

Scroll down.
A friend lays across more friends on a stranger's couch.
All of them dressed like death is a receipt:
something to press your dressed-up lips to
then discard.
They have stoplights for pupils.

If the couch were alive,
it would cough through busted ribs,
lose Q-tips in its nose,
would swallow mercury and glass.

CANS AND LOOSE POCKETS

We hardly take cabs into town,
too expensive, makes you gnaw
at the lip until your chapped wallet
bleeds to the red numbers rising.

Taxis sometimes swallow poets'
hearts, sometimes get you nearly there,
always barely light enough to crack
a can to pave the night.

Seems last night the backseat snatched
your plastic; picked a card any card.
The car's dark swung from window to window
as it cornered and all of the streetlights,

bike lights, and shop signs shined through.
I imagine the seatbelt pit, smooth shadow it was,
reached its hand into your goods, grabbed at
other gods and pulled. Dirty cavity, a treasure trove:

crumbs and small packs of paper,
bits of loose tobacco leaf, a stone
plucked from a wedding ring,
a bent pair of Ray Bans, a bit
and spiraled fingernail, a brand new
Chapstick, the last swig of courage
in a Remi Martin naggin.

You gave this alter a piece of you.

Prayed unknowingly, sang
demonically on the way home
as we stumbled back up George Street
with our haggard heads at our knees,
hoping the cracks in the Dublin stones
had any answer at all.

Part Three

Masks

IN BETWEEN

My mom sells houses
to people who have houses
but don't like their houses
or do like them
and want to sometimes live
in another house.
Soon, she will trade
keys and promises
for a large knife
to help gouge chunks from
her husband's medical bills,
buckets to drain
the sand from the gutters
around her house,
and a hammer
to chip at her son's
cement shoes
with Sally May stickers
on the heel.

My dad sells the word of God
but in a way that makes
Millennials shrug and
relentlessly agree.
He lives part-time with my mother
and part time at
the hospital.
His kidneys are always
somewhere between
purgatory and hell,
and his skin is thin
as Jesus' body on Sundays.
He'll make it through.

Sometimes it's all too
much but most times
it's just a matter of
rewording the prayer
or pushing the needle
past the scratch.

My sister once sold weed
between the North Truro cottages
but our dad
(her boss at the time)
found out and
fired her.
She rebelled and drew her body
into a tattooed dreamscape.
It resembles Cape Cod
if she fell asleep on the beach
reading Harry Potter
and her dreams
pushed out onto her skin.
I love her a lot.
I'm always proud of her
and when it rains where I am,
which is often,
I wonder
if it is raining where
she is too.
Sometimes to wait for the answer
is to touch the window
and tell myself
I feel the drops.

She smokes it more
than she sells it now
(purgatory)
and the sand dunes

in her backyard resemble
a lot of poorly buried things.
She didn't name her dog after me,
but we share a name
and she says she loves
the dumb little dude more
than anything in the world.

I don't know if God is sick of us or
we weren't communicating right,
but my Memé's last prayers
landed in my ears instead
when she said,
when she leaves me,
she only wants to spend eternity
in the in-between
where the clouds meet
the elevator doors.

Who the hell are we
to ask for the keys of heaven?
I couldn't grant her anything,
I'm not a god.
I try to listen
and try to bury stories like rubies,
but for the life of me,
I don't know how to hide
these growing piles of sand.

TO MOLD AND WRITHE

There was a dirt basement
into which the cat would slip to cough
or scratch rats. An unfinished porch
and the wood planks out
back that built it.

We lived atop the hill
on the edge of the
highway, orange groves to the north,
to the south, cow fields;
acres of what'd bake in the sun then
blow our way at the merciful tongue of the wind.
The highway always hummed the
way I would when I'd forgotten
the words to hymns.

I remember every awkward pause, how
it hung in the air outstretched like wrists. The
cascade of chins to chests; of eyes to darkness,
was enough of a boon to have allowed
my young eyes to potter down-pew. A
congregation frozen
in orison stranded a teen
mind to
mature or mold.
My unfinished prayer shoved
in the dirt and
the scratched rats, buried,
soon to writhe.

THE DROP

There is always a mirror behind the bar
to show you why you're there.
I pray out loud for fallen things.
That red angel. The whiskey snifter,
elbowed, tumbling.
A hurled empty bottle whipped end over end.
In all the worlds they shatter.
Seven years bad luck for a broken mirror.

Good mirrors hang heavy on nails
as if dared to be bumped.
As if an invisible cannon were strapped to its frame.
As you stare into it, you can hear the thin nail
bend behind the dusty you.

When I was younger, I punched things.
Bricks, trees, telephone poles.
Used to pockmark the hood of my car
when I was angry, little ditches, neatly pressed.
I would flash my knuckles at girls
or the football team,
show them my blues and reds
and blacks and laugh.
I don't do that anymore.

It quickly lost its humor and
once I learned what boys with angry
fists can do, I began keeping them in my pockets.
Held them there until they healed.
I learned to write my knuckles onto pages
or read them to an audience
or thumb them into a bottle and cork it.

I open my hands to catch things now.
That's my superpower.
If something falls, anything at all,
it's caught before it hits the ground.
Apples, forks, a wobbly nephew walking.
Put me in a room of mirrors.
Each one across from the other in a circle,
me in the middle.

Watch me watch me wait.
Watch me watch me stand tense.
Watch me watch me catch my breath.
Watch me watch me count.
Do the math in cursed years.
See me choose which me to save
as the soft nails creak from
the weight of worlds and cannons.

Of fallen angels and whiskey bottles.
I beg that I can still catch devils
and all types of glass
in a room full of scared boys. Watch me
watch me pray out loud,
reach for any answer, scramble
as I fumble prayer and terror
and keep them both off the ground
as I prime my skinny legs to pounce,
ready for the drop.

STAY INSIDE

I only go outside to
get groceries
or to run.
Other than that,
it rains knives.
I've mastered unlocking
doors with my elbow;
hand scrubbing has become
a wetness that burns.

The books on my shelf
throw knick-knacks
at me when I dig through
my phone.
I still need to dust.
When the internet isn't choppy
it is a frog nailed to a wall.
When the dishes aren't clean,
they sink.

The tree outside my only window
sheds on everything,
now everyone on my block
has itchy eyes and a cough.
Gods in hazmat suits
removed three people
from my street this week.
When I touch things,
I cut off my hand.

When the rain comes
it kills street sleepers
and leaves thick blades
upright in windscreens.

Everyone counts days like commandments
1. Thou shalt not breathe deep.
12. Thou shalt be burdens under thine own roof.
24. If thou touch thine eyes,
you gotta pluck those fuckers out.

We are learning to pray
with our heads in bags,
with our gloved hands
tied behind our backs.

These days,
death is on every tongue
and we are but lost
and thirsty fools.

OCEAN HELD STILL

The Atlantic is a thick blanket of glass.
My first few steps were a moth's wings.
Half a whale's tale
rooted above the ground
now greets me miles past.
My feet land solid
and all of New England
is a loose-leaf page on a mirror.
I trust it less as I go.

My mother would cook us anything
we wanted for our birthdays.
It's hard to remember
the smells anymore.
Can't taste much.
I'm sure they were splendid.
I look back.
New England is wiped away.

If she ever found
I'd lost my memories
she would surely crumble;
my father too,
and most of my lovers.
I know she is a
passionate woman.
I'd like to imagine
she cooked up a storm.

I like to think they lined up
around the block to get a bowlful.
I bet the towns kids
waddled home fat as seagulls

and dad still had
leftovers for tomorrow.
I don't believe I've drowned yet,
I don't think.

I like a story
where they kiss each other goodnight.
Once after their teeth were brushed
and again, on the nose
when one would start to
fade away.

CAW

The sun sprawled out across the lake
like a sprung guitar string.
Northwood sounded a low note. My father
and I paddled kayaks in no particular direction;
two sober birds on a drunken pilot's flight plan.

I asked if he'll be alright,
I was the soft pale of wrists.
He opened to speak and a crow tumbled out. It hit
the water, floated crooked at the surface.

He wiped his chin and a carp pulled the body under.
Mom would be home in an hour.
She left work early to watch me be her son again
before I flew home, away from them.

My father cupped a swallow
of the lake into his hands
and brought it to his lips.

I write pretty words from my apartment,
cross them out, and scratch again.
An ocean splits the distance between my parents
and me. This ocean has a light calm at times

but rages in the dark;
it collects dead birds and dropped planes the way
pilots hide their empty naggins in the bin.

PURGE

"Would you say there's any end in sight, Charlie?"
    "I'd say you nearly have an answer to that question already Maurice."
                    -Kevin Barry, *Nightboat to Tangier.*

I packed my car with the picture of my uncle shaking the
president's hand
            my baseball card collection
            the tin cup of bolts
            the jar of shells
            bags of books I'd never read,
            the box of ones I had.

        My molded pillow spotted brown with sweat drops
like bee stings.
            A can of empty pens
            a couple pens, abandoned, and
            my old flip phone.

In the glove box, buried my college degree and all my baby
teeth,
            I released the emergency break
            and pushed the cart into the lake.

I dug a hole in the backyard,
            dragged my winter chest down the stairs
            with unnerving thumps, opened it,
            and dumped my scarves, mittens,
            my woolen hats into the pit.

I tossed my writing desk from the second-floor window
            onto the pile.   A leg snapped
            and the corner dug into the dirt.

I broke my laptop over my knee
and flung the pieces in.

Flipped my mattress across the top
and set the mess ablaze.

There was more smoke than flame and I watched it grow
a tangled wig of devils up the trees.

CALL THE LOCKSMITH

Outside, a siren rounds and ebbs through town.
Nobody knows what this means.
In the Midwest (Oklahoma, Dolly Parton, meth),
that same sound rattles through livestock
and the locals move to cover,
watch pregnant clouds spin-on
as they genuflect and tongue psalms.

The siren climbs our spines,
nestles in our ears,
itches.

All the bars have spit us out and
apartments swallowed us whole.

A slender black house cat struts
every sidewalk on the planet.
Links its way through fence posts
and slips through window cracks.

Rubs its neck on every
doorknob and neighbor.
Makes us lay one rigor mortis body
between us and every other body.

6 feet is a brother
is a science teacher
is a movie star
is a casket.

This cat has chewed up all our toilet paper,
has buried our soap
and raked our bones.
Has hollered from the street corner
and from every balcony in Venice.
Has drowned businesses.
Has gutted towns.
Has burned chests.
Has washed sounds.

This slender beast has reset the clock.
Has snapped the key in every lock.

THINGS WE BLINDLY TAKE AS GOSPEL

When I was younger, I said words
because they sounded cool,
but didn't always get them right.
Or got them right but didn't really "get them".
When I was in elementary school,
I learned all the words to Alanis Morisette's
Jagged Little Pill album, minus the curse words
that my mom conveniently coughed over.

Through the years, words gained traction,
meant more to me in weight and style.
"Acrosst" became "Across".
"No Problem" turned to "Absolutely".
"Hate" became superfluous
and "Love" stayed "Love" since there
doesn't seem to be enough
and it's meant to coat towns like snowfall.

My favorite curse word is Motherfucker.
Where the emphasis is on the *Fuck*.
The word holds no literal weight
but the sentiment still carries
its power over language gaps.

MotherFUCKer!

Hear those broad shoulders.
Feel the lips pop,
the tip of the tongue flick,
the bite of the bottom lip,
                    (fff),
the dam of the tongue against
the roof of your mouth,

and the guttural punch to finish it off.

Mo-ther-FUCK-er.
What a catch.

I've danced with glittery bald-headed pop stars
at the Sulkiest Lounge in Portland.
A Madonna impersonator taught me not to
say you're sorry unless you mean it
and if someone apologizes to you,
to accept it only if you do.

This world is a catacomb of assumptions.
Things we blindly take as gospel
like the morality behind police or
the benefits of recycling.
We never question what we know
and hide stars the moment we collect them.

We pick them from between the trees
and out of television screens
then stuff them in our pockets before we see
if they're made of plastic.
Be a sanctuary of scholastics.
Press all the things you think you know
into a shiny golden coin
then test its durability between your teeth.

See which folk tales turn into dust
and which ones crack your motherfucking jaw.

HOIT ROAD MARSH WHEN THE COLD CREPT IN

The moon hung over the pond
like a fat stone had caught air
on a good skip and stuck there.
The water rippled towards the car,
licked the road's edge then drug
       itself
       back.

Green numbers on the radio began to fade
as the battery drained.
Our breath turned to crystals
that spread across the windows.
Stars I remember thinking.

We knew how to take up space.
We didn't know shit
on how to maneuver the cold
the dark, the buckles, the clips, the hands,
the mouth, the teeth, the slick, the wheel,
the curfew, the belt, the heights, the accents,
the cars, their passing lights, the flags,
our youth, the warmth, the teeth,
the teeth, dear god, the teeth.

LOCKS AND LATCHES

Sometimes it's a bed in a shoebox
with a price tag made of gold.
Sometimes it's the woven
tea cozy walls of a poem.
Sometimes it's a kitchen billowing
with the scent of warm food
and your mother's voice in song.

It's a warehouse in Galway
where artists leave their hearts
in shavings on the concrete walls
and the concrete floor and
we sip good coffee on the couch.

It's a small town in California where the sunset
can be an open wound but the sky's been through
heavier smoke than that and is happy
to sit and laugh with you about it.

We all find home where we do
and know in our guts where it isn't.

Sometimes we aren't sure
if the doorknob
will chill or warm
our hand,
but we sure as hell know
the weight of it,
know the creak of the clocks

and the walls inside,
but we pray to locks
and latches that it still
knows and wants to
warm our bones.

We know the sound
the door makes
when it opens,
know the crash
a door makes
when it shuts.

UMBRELLAS

Open an umbrella inside and your
grandmother will lose all of her hair.
If it is opened in the rain, the wind
will snap its brittle metal fingers back.

The rain, they say, is made of acid,
sands down gravestones in the park.
Somebody's baby or a grandfather's
proud name fades with time.

Rain plucks knives from the air, splats soft,
carves up everything drop by drop.
As a kid, I'd jar my head back,
open my mouth like an upturned umbrella.

I'd catch the water how I could, it
would gather at the mercy of the rain's pace.
I would wait and soak and soak heavy,
collecting, what I imagined was clean water
on my tongue and swallowing knives.

As an adult, I wrap the top layer tight,
walk strong, succumb to the weather and wear
the cumbersome like a good scar story.
I smile when I think of their faces.
When I see where I'm supposed to be, I run.

FOR THOSE WHO DIDN'T THINK THEY'D
OUTLIVE ME
Or
WHEN I DIE

After Ryan McLellan

I tried to write a poem about the time
I found God in an apple core,
but that never actually happened.
We haven't talked in years.
Not for lack of trying,
I just had the phone on silent,
still do.

It's always in my pocket
or it's always in my hand but
She's one of those I know
will always call again tomorrow.
I'm physically so far away
from everyone who's gotten me here.

I wish good things in their direction.
A free drink that leads to a new friend,
a good dog that greets you on the street,
your housemate does the dishes
or your lover changed the sheets.
You catch yourself smiling without reason.

If I die in my sleep in a shoebox in Dublin,
God will show up like,
"Dude, have you been ghosting me?"
Then we'll laugh at the irony.

She'll reach out for me
because things with wings

tend to forgive easily.
I'll reach for my phone
without thinking
and my hand will go right through.
It will blink in the dark
the way apples,
through an orchard,
drop.

Notifications
from people who knew for sure
I'd outlive them.

I won't respond,
but I'll pluck an angel feather
from my back
and write a poem
on my forearm
on the way out.
I'll revise it on the way there
and read it to strangers in a dive bar
or wherever it is
that angels take you
when they finally take you.

GATE 7

It will start with two people at a gate,
waiting for the plane to open its belly.
They will sit with three seats between them,
a habit like washing your hands or
locking the door with your arm in your sleeve.

People will begin to stroll in by ones
then threes then hoards;
nervous bodies filling gaps.
The first two to embrace will be a dropped vase.
Folks will cringe; step back, careful not to catch
porcelain shards or breathe death.

Slowly, elbows will bump, and strangers will say
"It's still all a bit crazy, isn't it?"
Then a few from the back will laugh
and a toddler will cry, and a young mother will rock
her because it's all she knows, so far, to do,
and everyone will remember being all of them.

The elderly will watch
from the roped off corner,
warding demons with their eyes
behind hospital masks.

When they begin to board,
people will forget
that other people were poison.
They will line up out of order

the way they always had.
Some will get frustrated
for comfort's sake.

When the first plane flies,
it will be full as a hospital
or a concert hall on Christmas.

It will lift with strength or magic,
the way it always had,
sewing the clouds together,
writing letters in the sky.

QUIET TONGUE
From a Nymph named Echo

I wanted, once, to swallow mossy stones,
to muffle out my voice. Instead, I stepped
over your body and walked into the hills.

The trees here grow as high as birds fly.
The fields are open blankets
lush with flowers, bees, and grain.
I sometimes put my lips to the river's top
and let its whispers form in there.

In these hills, my lungs are free to breathe
the way they know themselves to do.
I house a quiet tongue
and place a honeysuckle on it.

ACKNOWLEDGEMENTS:

I am lucky enough to say that my family has loved me wherever I've gone, and I know this with my whole heart. Thank you, mom, dad, and SunMi. Thank you to my incredible partner Katie, and her loving family. This book wouldn't have been possible without my poetry family, Wil, Ryan, Anna, Hazel, Emmet, Conor, Molly, Niamh, Aideen, the 2 Meter Review, and the Glasshouse Poetry crew. Thank you to the All-Ireland Poetry Slam, University College Cork's Creative Writing Program, Burren College of Art, Niamh Regan, Dead Horse Jive, The Roisin Dubh, and every herald song that fumbled from our mouths or tumble we took from Eyre Square to Spanish Arch to Ruxton Court: our first slice of heaven.

Please visit these sites and become familiar with their work. If you have the means, please consider supporting these organizations. Their work is crucial in the fight for equality and justice and helping build a better world.

www.blacklivesmatter.com
www.nowhitesaviors.org
www.aapd.com
www.swopusa.org
www.thetaskforce.org
www.narf.org
www.marshap.org
www.theokraproject.com

Photo by Julia Monard

Beau Williams (He, Him) is an American poet, workshop facilitator, and spoken word artist based in Dublin, Ireland. Williams' poetry style has been described as joyful, heart-wrenching, and captivating. His work focuses on issues of the heart – exploring the complexity of human relationships, inspiring hope in the face of darkness, and generally interrogating the way that we occupy space in this world.

He has two collections: Nail Gun and a Love Letter (Swimming with Elephants Publication) and now Things I Blindly Took As Gospel (Waterside Publication). He has a Masters in Creative Writing from the University College of Cork and was the 2018/2019 All Ireland Poetry Slam Champion. In response to the 2020 COVID pandemic, Williams started the 2 Meter Review Literary Journal and the Virtual Poetry Marketplace. Feel free to contact him and say hello at beauwilliamspoet@gmail.com or find him at beauwilliamspoet.com.

www.ingramcontent.com/pod-product-compliance
Lightning Source LLC
LaVergne TN
LVHW011426080426
835512LV00005B/290